# WHAT PEOPLE ARE SAYING...

*Reading Barbara Joyce is like sitting with a sage, who you intuitively know has been where you are and traveled many roads to cross paths with you now. Quickly, she becomes a confidante, and you trust her instincts. As she invites you into her world, you are enriched in full measure. The gift she brings is a commerce far beyond the exchange of money. It is the timeless, and universal, value of wisdom.*

*This is a book about healing. It addresses an integral need human beings share that is entwined in our DNA. We call it security. Although my colleague probably did not intend to write a panacea, her method for introspection is just that. In five steps, she guides you to bridge the honesty gap between your head and your heart. With each step unconscious fears that once troubled your heart and confused your head, evaporate as quickly as they were formed. The result is freedom to be the real you.*

*When Barbara writes, "By committing just one hour a day to your growth and development, you will need a telescope to look back at your life by the end of the coaching term," I believe her, and so can you.*

*For anyone who has ever felt lost, exhausted, or overwhelmed by life, Barbara Joyce lifts you out of the overwhelm of the endless info-age into the clear light of soul understanding.*

— Barbara Condron, author of *Master Living and
Spiritual Renaissance*

*Barbara Joyce is an excellent coach and personal development expert. Barbara brings enthusiasm and an uncommon degree of optimism and positive energy. Her energy alone has been fuel for my own journey! It has been a true gift to work with and learn from such a wonderful person. I would recommend her coaching or mastermind program to anyone who seeks to change their personal or professional circumstances or results. The change in my own life has been profound since I began working with Barbara, and while a lot of guidance came from the Universe, it was Barbara's approach that put me in touch with it.*

— Rhonda Magee, Senior Consultant at
Garden Hill Consulting, LLC


*This book offers practical and straightforward advice on the why and the how of finding a life coach. Barbara's own story offers inspiration and hope for anyone seeking to make positive changes for a more fulfilling life.*

— K. Granger


*I have had the honor of watching Barbara live the truth of the words she shares on these pages. The eloquence with which she communicates the power awaiting anyone ready to do the work is magical in its composition—a must read!*

— Dan Mangena, CEO Dreamer HQ Inc.

*Barbara has had many life challenges and the change that has taken place in Barbara's life has been amazing. Everything she shares and talks about is 100% true in so many of our lives today. This book will inspire and help you find your own place in life. She is on top now and ready to help you as well.*

— Chad Reynolds, Unlock Wealth Creator

*Barbara Joyce embodies what it is like to live from your authentic power. Her book will lead you to your true destiny—a deep and abiding relationship with your Self.*

— Stacy Oliver, Publisher,
*MIND BODY SOUL MAGAZINE*

*This book should be called "Brilliance by Barbara"! So many authors add a bunch of fluff to make a book longer or to try and "sell" a client. Not Barbara. The advice is clear, concise, honest, and direct. Kudos to you Ms. Joyce for your commitment to others!*

— Allan Susoeff, Jr., PE, PhD, Mentor,
and Coach at AskAlHow.com

*I read the first four pages and I'm hiring Barbara as my Life Coach. This is first book I've read that's honest, to the point and results driven.*

— Christine Hepler, Feng Shui Consultant

*Barbara's willingness, tenacity, courage and determination to live her very best version of herself through personal growth & development is infectious & inspirational to all who choose this path!! Having the privilege & honor of coaching her, I can wholeheartedly say, "She's the Real Deal" and her passion, authenticity, and growth shines brightly through on every page!! Well done!*

— Tina Perrmann, Intuitive Life Coach & Mentor

*Your internal image is where your power originates. Barbara's book beautifully illustrates how working with a life coach can elevate your self-image and actions to meet your goals and dreams.*

— Caren Libby, Image Media, LLC

*"Ditch the Boyfriend" —read the book and find a way to work with Barbara Joyce! She knows the way because she has been there. This book will start you on the path to anything and everything you want to create!*

— Shawn Feurer, The Universal Mindset Disruptor

*Barbara has laid out a beautiful and simple coach "playbook" using her life experiences, if this book doesn't cause you to evaluate the "game of life" you are playing nothing will!!.*

— Pamela Martin, Life Scientist,
Metamorphosismind.com

*Barbara has really hit a home run with this book! I can resonate with every page as she brings out her truth, opens her heart to belief and faith, and shares her courage to become her deeply desired "best self." It is ALL captured so well. When facing adversity, don't run away—sprint towards it.*

— Karen Fiorini , Senior Inner Circle Coach & Mentor, Proctor Gallagher Institute

*This book will encourage you to be the best version of yourself.*

— L. McDaniel

*I'll never forget that day in my backyard garage I was working on your black Honda Civic. You were telling me about Bob Proctor and how his program was life changing. I could tell that you wholeheartedly believed in his program and it was obvious you were getting into coaching because you truly wanted to help others.*

*Knowing you helped to break down my "terror barrier" —I knew I needed a coach, but I was too scared to hire anyone. My life has completely changed for the better since I've consistently been working with a coach. I love how much you truly care about going after your dreams and helping others go after theirs. You're an inspiration to so many! Anyone that works with you is blessed!*

— David Marks, ASE Certified Master technician, CEO Quality Auto STL

*A wonderful, easy to follow guide for making profound improvement in the quality of your life. It's a great read for women AND men who are searching to discover the simplicity of achieving their desires and dreams. Since meeting Barbara, my life has not been the same. Soon after meeting and listening to her, I began to experience how easy and almost automatic it was to fill my emptiness with joyous things—that which I had given up putting any energy into trying to accomplish in the past. We could all use a coach to help us easily navigate a more enjoyable and rewarding life.*

— Bill Barger, CEO, Firstline Merchant Services Inc.

*I've known Barbara as a client, fellow coach, and most importantly as a friend. I always find great value in our exchanges, regardless of the context or relationship. Barbara is a powerhouse of a teacher and guide, and I know you will find great value in reading this book. She has done an awesome job delivering how, why, and when to get a life coach so you get more powerful results, easier and faster than you can alone.*

— Mike Kitko, Executive Coach, Speaker, Author

*This book is an easy guide to help you find a life coach who best fits your life and your desires. Barbara keeps it real and simple—definitely a great start for those who are wanting more out of their life.*

— J. Jarecki

*Barbara Joyce is an extremely important person in my life. She has spent years doing her own work and can now share her wisdom with the rest of us. She is upbeat, positive and compassionate. She has the ability to make us feel good as she gently guides us out of the emotional quagmire, we all create for ourselves. Through her life coaching and mastermind programs, I have learned so much about myself and those around me. She is a treasure.*

— Kristin Antony, Nurse Practitioner

*Barbara´s vulnerability, ability to make complicated things simple, and outstanding way of writing gets you hooked in the first few pages. She teaches you something you've probably never thought about: how to find the perfect life coach. This book is a MUST!*

— Adela Martinez Camacho

*Finding purpose and serenity should be our mission in life; when asking for directions, ask directions of someone that knows how to get you to where you want to go. Barbara knows how to do just that! "How insignificant mere money-seeking looks in comparison with a serene life—a life that dwells in the ocean of Truth, beneath the waves, beyond the reach of tempests, in the Eternal Calm!" (James Allen).*

— Randy Eikermann, CPA/PFS, CFP®,
Eikermann & Associates, LLC

*Barbara Joyce is what I often refer to as a "Change Agent" or Agent of Change. Through her private groups, Modern Women Rising and its associated Radical Rising program, she has shown us what "intentional living" looks like when you focus on your passions, gifts, talents, and strengths. Her open, honest communication and teaching encourages you to join her personal mission to build positive change in your business and in the world, and most importantly "within yourself" by doing the inner work and changing your mindset.*

*The inner work she shares (and she herself practices daily) creates "magical" change, "magical" love, and an awareness of ALL that you are. You are then able to be the light of hope and peace which attracts others into this community for positive change. The women Barbara touches with her program will leave a lasting impact in our world for generations to come.*

*Thank you so very much Barbara Joyce for shining your beacon of light so brightly that I was able to find, participate, and collaborate with you in your personal mission initiatives. The benefits gained have been beyond measure in helping me develop new patterns, habits, and tools to live life fully in the "present"...authentically with no apologies.*

*Ditch The Boyfriend and Get a Life Coach is an inspiring must-read. I found myself not wanting to put this book down. Barbara is smart, witty, fun, and fully authentic about what it takes to make a positive change in one's life. She truly holds you accountable as you achieve all that you desire for your life.*

— Michele Petralia, Owner, CeleBRAte Her Style, and
contributing author to *Fearless and Fabulous*

*As a former client and now a friend of Barbara's, I am impressed by the level of vulnerability that she displays in this book. It is testament to how much she cares about everyone winning at the game of life. She is open and honest. She provides insights and tools. Most of all she presents this book with gratitude, as she has lived it first-hand.*

— Mike Huxford

*Watching Barbara evolve over the years into a dynamic and energetic Life Coach has been an amazing journey. This must-read, Ditch the Boyfriend and Get a Life Coach, is a raw telling of the true story behind the strong, growing woman that I have come to know. How one change in your life can bring about a string of remarkable changes is told through this powerful account of her hard work and determination.*

— Barb Wagner, Independent Business Consultant and Artist

*Barbara Joyce's passion for life coaching and how it can benefit anyone shines through in this book. By sharing her own life experience, Barbara demonstrates how a connection with the right life coach can empower you to unlock your own potential and help guide you to the success of your dreams!*

— Emily Appleton, MPAS, PA-C

In her story, my little sis has captured the essence of how someone from a typical traditional family can end up a broken and lost individual. I've had the pleasure of seeing her go from an unhappy, non-focused, and dissatisfied person to a truly happy, powerful, and purpose-driven woman. While her journey was tough at times, she has evolved into the person I want to grow up to be (as a 65 year old)! Admiration and pride are insufficient words for how I feel about the growth I've seen with Barbara's (Beebletob's) tremendous transformation. We can all learn from how she conquered and excelled in Life following what she has shared here. Good Luck to all on your journey! Love you Beebletobs!

— Big Sis, Sue

*Ditch the Boyfriend and Get a Life Coach* is an engaging and easy to read reminder that you can make permanent and constructive changes in yourself. As her mother, it is amazing to see the transformation that has taken place in Barbara's life since beginning to work with a life coach…and an even bigger change as she began to share her own work.

— Bert Schinzing, Mom and Fan

"Wanted" Amazing Life! This is your guide. Thank you Barbara, for simplifying the complicated journey of achieving life's goals!

— Vivi Radtke

# DITCH THE BOYFRIEND

# AND GET A
# LIFE
# COACH

## TRANSFORM YOUR LIFE FROM TOXIC CO-DEPENDENCY TO AUTHENTIC COURAGE

### BARBARA JOYCE

# Ditch the Boyfriend and Get a Life Coach

Transform Your Life from Toxic Codependency to Authentic Courage

Barbara Joyce

Joyce Publications

Published by Joyce Publications, Laguna Beach, CA

Project Management and Book Design: Davis Creative Publishing Partners, CreativePublishingPartners .com

Editor: Cheryl Roberts

Illustrator: Adela Martinez Camacho

Publisher's Cataloging-In-Publication Data
(Prepared by The Donohue Group, Inc.)

Names: Joyce, Barbara, 1969- author.
Title: Ditch the boyfriend and get a life coach : transform your life from toxic co-dependency
        to authentic courage / Barbara Joyce.
Description: Laguna Beach, CA : Joyce Publications, [2022]
Identifiers: ISBN 9798985515701 (paperback) | ISBN 9798985515718 (ebook)
Subjects: LCSH: Personal coaching. | Women--Life skills guides. | Courage. | Codependency.
        | Self-esteem in women. | Social comparison. | LCGFT: Self-help publications. | BISAC:
        BODY, MIND & SPIRIT / Inspiration & Personal Growth. | FAMILY & RELATIONSHIPS /
        Divorce & Separation. | SELF-HELP / Codependency.
Classification: LCC BF637.P36 J63 2022 (print) | LCC BF637.P36 (ebook) | DDC 158.3--dc23

        2022

## Dedication

*To my sister Sue, this one's for you.*

*And for anyone
on the verge of a spiritual awakening—
your world is ready and waiting.*

# TABLE OF CONTENTS

# FOREWORD

People all over our planet are waking up to the truth that there is a great destiny loaded and coded within us all. People are becoming aware that their fate is not in the hands of external forces, environment, or decisions made by younger versions of themselves that may have set them on an unfavorable path.

And more and more individuals are becoming aware of another truth: our life experiences are determined by our beliefs, mental programming, and perceptions that then turn themselves into our life experiences.

Picking up *Ditch the Boyfriend and Get a Life Coach* indicates that you are ready to wake up to the endless possibilities that are available to you. In fact, you are ready to consciously participate in your destiny while releasing excuses about why you'll never be able to achieve the happiness, health, success, or prosperity you once dreamed of.

I have had several mentors in my lifetime, so I know the tremendous impact the right coach or mentor can have in your life. They see things in you that you can't see for yourself, and they know how to bring the best of you to the surface. They see the real you.

I agree wholeheartedly with what Barbara says in this book: *"The journey toward your fulfillment is not on a path you walk alone."* Everyone has a "greater vision" within them. However, it's extremely difficult to keep developing your limitless potential without someone who can help you shift your perception of the world, of yourself, and what you are capable of.

This book will assist you in developing a better understanding of what life coaching is and how it can help you. It will also help you determine if you're ready for a life coach and how to find one that is right for you.

If you're ready to believe in your dreams again and become the best possible you, Barbara lays out powerful truths about how you can create the life you really want. Now, it's up to you. To your success!

– Bob Proctor, Bestselling Author of *You Were Born Rich*

# IN CELEBRATION

Bob Proctor
1934 – 2022

After hearing of Bob Proctor's recent passing, I do the only thing that comes to mind. Which is to share in celebrating this amazing man's life and Legend!

I am very grateful for meeting Bob Proctor, for being introduced to his teachings, for his mentorship, and for this selfie!

Let me explain more. I had the rare opportunity of being in this man's Presence. And when that happened, my whole life changed.

I first learned of Bob's teachings through another coach. Then I learned more from Arash Vossoughi who helped introduce me to programs and events to get me in his Presence.

I attended these events virtually and in person and decided that I wanted to teach Bob's material. I signed up to work directly with Bob Proctor and to learn from the best teacher and mentor on human development and potential, a choice I will never regret.

As a PGI consultant along with my own programs, I help facilitate and develop the potential in others that is waiting to be recognized and released. I cannot be more proud of the work that myself and all the other PGI consultants are doing throughout the world to carry on Bob Proctor's legacy.

At one event at Bob's home, I had another opportunity to be face to face with him. In true Barbara (at the time) fashion, I asked for a selfie!

I could have asked anything of him...guidance, support, a quick question to learn more...but his Presence in a picture is what I chose.

I guess I have been a little enamored with his life and what he has done. But also asking for that selfie was just a way for me to connect with him on a different (and fun) level.

What I value most is human connection. Understanding and Love flowing from one to the other is what this picture represents to me. The flowing of a mutual bond of our belief in humanity and our ability to do good in the world.

Today, I say thank you Bob Proctor for being in my life and blessing me in ways I never thought possible.

By committing to changing my thoughts daily, my life has elevated in ways I could not have previously imagined. Today I believe in humanity and our evolution. I am incredibly grateful and humbled to share with others what was passed along to me.

Much love.

*Barbara*

# Introduction

This book is truly dedicated to the old me, and any person like the old me, who:

- Fell into life accidentally and hoped, somehow, "it" would all work out
- Wanted something more but had no clue how to get it
- Woke up and felt as if she were living someone else's life (I was)
- Felt there was more to life, that there was a purpose, but was uncertain how to find it
- Was asleep and had to wake up in order to come alive

If you are like this old me, stuck but hoping life will somehow offer you more, this is your wake-up call. Your life can and will offer you more, but only when you start offering more to life.

Life is full of endless possibilities. Although you may not be where you want to be today, and perhaps you've made some mistakes in the past, you *can* change into the person you are meant to be.

You are smart and talented enough to do anything you set your mind to. Your dreams are there, hanging in the balance, waiting for you to set clear intentions then follow through with appropriate actions.

Because this book is dedicated to the old me, it is written in the voice of an upper-class woman struggling to find her place. However, this book has timeless advice that will resonate with anyone drowning in an ocean of past conditioning, knowing intuitively that if they dive deep and resurface, they can reach their illusive safe harbor.

The purpose of this book is to guide any girl, teenager, or woman (or anyone, for that matter) who:

- Is caught in the crossfire of adversity and can't find her way out
- Knows she is unique but keeps striving to fit in
- Is lost in the "I can't" and "I'm not good enough" mindset by continually comparing herself to what she sees in others
- Thinks what she wants out of life is out of reach
- Is stuck in a loop of negative behavior and can't stop
- Is mired in a relationship that is toxic and doesn't have the heart to leave

If you are ready to walk away from these scenarios and embrace a life of freedom, then you have come to the right place. Here you will learn to replace the evil whisper of self-doubt with a clear message of belief in yourself. Here you will learn the truth about yourself, starting with this:

- You were put on this planet at this particular time for a particular purpose that only you can fulfill *because* you are the only *you* in the universe

- No matter what you have been through, your past does not define your future

- You can have the life you want no matter what is going on around you, if you are willing to follow certain steps

If this sounds interesting, then you, my dear, are in for a treat. It is time to brush yourself off, stand up tall, and go show this world what you are made of! It is time to learn how to live an authentic, intentional, purposeful life.

Chapter One

# LIFE IS A GAME

I'm familiar with the phrase, "Life is a game; all you have to do is know how to play it." Sounds reasonable to me. Every game I have ever played has come with instructions. For example, the board game LIFE clearly states the objective: "Collect money and LIFE tiles and have the highest dollar amount at the end of the game." It also comes with setup instructions, tips on how to play, and even how to win.

So, where are our instructions for winning at our game of real life? Some find it in religious practices and beliefs, some find it in achieving economic goals, and many others are still trying to figure out the meaning of the game.

Until I turned 48, I had spent my life trying to play the game *the right way, the winning way*. I was a good kid who got good grades. I was athletic and talented. I graduated from high school and college, and even went on to earn a master's degree. I got married, had three children, and got a good job.

I was following the rules of the game of life as they were taught to me: work hard, get a job, have a family, raise your kids, hope to retire, and then die.

I was a rule follower, and, from the outside, I looked like I was winning at the game of life. But inside, I didn't feel like I was winning. Inside, I knew I was meant for more. Inside, there was a yearning for the life I had dreamed of as a child, the one that I still visited when I closed my eyes and allowed my imagination to wander. In this dream life, I was the heroine of my story, and I teamed up with my best friend to fight the evil in the world.

When I closed my eyes, I would go back to that time when my best friend and I would pretend all day long. Our imaginations were vibrant, strong, full of possibilities. We had not yet subscribed to the belief that there was anything we could *not* do. So, we ruled the world we imagined.

Our favorite game was Witches' Trail. In this game, we set out on our adventure on Witches' Trail! The trail was in our backyard, a beautifully landscaped garden surrounded by Carolina azaleas. The object of the game was to make it to the end of the trail without being captured by the witches; however, we not only had to avoid the witches, but we also had to recognize them and lock them up so they couldn't hurt anyone else.

We were the adventurers, the good guys, the heroines of this game. We relied on our instincts to lead us in the right direction and to sniff out where the evil witches were hiding. And we always won! The witches were conquered. In this childhood game, we saved ourselves and the rest of the world from the witches.

Then something awful happened to me. I lost my ability to believe I could conquer evil and adversity. I lost the vibrancy of my youthful, creative power. I lost the wonder of that empowered girl. I was no longer a young girl who ruled her world. I was a woman that had been handed a new set of rules.

During my formative adult years, I read every book, participated in self-help programs, committed and recommitted myself to my husband and my children, and threw myself into my work. I prayed, I hired counselors, fired counselors, hired new ones. I followed every lead that I thought would guide me to a fulfilled life, only to end up exhausted and overwhelmed.

The new rules said I was not capable in my own right, that in order to be whole, I needed a man, so I should look *outside* myself for myself. Then I was taught that the men in my life knew more than the women, and especially, that *the* man in my life knew more about what I needed than what *I* knew or felt. Which seemed to work—right up until it didn't.

I lost my marriage. I lost my job. Suddenly the rules of the game of life were all wrong. Or I had been wrong. Or both? What would it take for me to win now that I had lost?

The more curious I became, the more I searched, the more I was confused.

The divorce turned out to be a blessing in disguise because it reignited my determination to find what really worked! Determined not to fail again, I went in search of, no surprises here, the perfect mate. If I could just find the "right man," I would certainly win!

The story most women are told by society is that in order to live happily ever after, we need to get married and have children, mind our manners, sit up straight, look pretty, and be kind. Furthermore, being kind includes accommodating others' needs and wants, even if it goes against our values and instincts.

So, I kept applying the same rules I had followed that lost me the game the first time. I failed to see that playing by the rules I was taught would not allow me to win, that the rules in that instruction manual would not coach me to be a winner. It could instruct me on how to be a wife, mother, daughter, but not to go inside myself to find my purpose. I needed a different instruction manual if I wanted to find my winning streak.

I was unable to see what I had been able to see before. It was the children's game—the fanciful, made-up Witches' Trail—that actually held the secret to my life: my instincts, my playfulness, my perceptions, my friendships.

I failed to see the bigger truth, that we are all born perfect. Then we deny our magic. We forget our power. We lose touch with who we really are. We deny our right to win on our own terms and, instead, seek someone to provide what we believe we cannot provide for ourselves.

We look to men—rich men, handsome men, skinny men, tall men, men who are available and men who aren't—expecting to find our financial security, emotional security, and sometimes even our spiritual security. It took me going all the way down this rabbit hole of looking for love in all the wrong places to learn that looking for someone else to make me feel whole is not a winning game plan at all.

If this is you and, like me, you know that you have a role in this world but don't know how or where to find it, you need to do what I was finally able to do: ditch the boyfriend and get a life coach.

## Why?

Let's take this life is a game analogy to a whole new level. Let's suppose for a minute that life truly is just a game. You may have had some wins and losses throughout the years. But right now, despite wanting to win more than anything, you are not having a winning streak.

If you are determined to win—but that is not your current reality—do you fire the players or the coach?

In professional team sports, a combination of the two is often done. They fire some of the athletes and sometimes they fire the coach, too. But with professional athletes engaged in an individual sport, the athlete can't be fired.

The athlete is the team and the key ingredient. What these individual athletes do when they are not winning is hire a new coach! They do not keep putting their faith in the coach that isn't working for them.

In your game of life, *you* are the individual athlete in this sport. So, naturally, what you need is a new coach! It's that simple.

Yet what I see all too often is that we fire *ourselves*. When we do that, we give up our dreams. We accept where we are, find as much happiness as we can muster in that perceived inevitable situation, and we push through, accepting unhappiness and complacency as our destiny. We resign ourselves to the idea that those big dreams are for other people.

I want you to really understand how ridiculous this is. It would be akin to Serena Williams having walked off the court after losing the first set in the 2009 Wimbledon semi-finals, saying to herself, "I lost one set. It's too hard and will take too long to win now, so why bother?" Serena, with her indomitable fighting spirit, would never have done that.

What we really need to let go of is all the negative talk. We need to stop beating ourselves up for past errors and press on in the face of adversity. And we need to dig down deep for self-discipline, self-respect, and self-realization!

But we don't. We accept less from ourselves and, eventually, we quit dreaming altogether.

It's really sad when this happens. I know because it happened to me. I had accepted my failing marriage as the best option for myself, lived my life for my kids, and went to a job every day that was unfulfilling, just to make ends meet.

I did finally wake up but not the easy way. I finally figured out that if I was the predominant player in my life, I needed to start winning.

How? You guessed it. I got a new coach!

## It's time to ask yourself four important questions:

1. Have you fired yourself?
2. Have you accepted less than your best in your daily life?
3. Are you living and working for others but ultimately forgetting yourself?
4. Have you given up on your dream, or worse, just quit dreaming altogether?

If you answered yes to any of these questions, then it is time to reevaluate your life. It is time to shake things up and find the power to win!

You may think you aren't meant to win at this game of life. Maybe you believe you are supposed to be reasonably happy and content with what you've got.

Well, guess what? Whatever you believe is what is true for you *today*.

But what if, like me, you wonder—*really* wonder—whether your dreams were given to you for a reason. And you have a feeling somewhere inside that you do have a purpose in this world. Can you hear that tiny but persistent voice telling you there is more to life? Isn't it about time you found out?

Say yes! Then get ready to approach your life in different ways than you have before. Start by considering who your "coach" has been up until this point:

- Unconscious habits
- Behaviors that limit your potential
- Your family dictating what you should or should not do
- A doctor telling you to take this pill or that drug
- A therapist who tried to help by rehashing past or present unsatisfactory situations

Whatever or whoever your coach has been, if you don't feel like a winner, then I have a secret for you: you've picked the wrong coach. If you had the right coach, you would be winning, or feeling you are on the right track to win. If you had the right coach, you wouldn't have bought this book. (Wink.)

## So, right now, ask yourself these questions:

- What if I found a different approach to life that allowed me to win?
- What if I found an approach to life that permitted my dreams to become reality?
- What if I found something that not only enabled me to find my true purpose, but also entitled me to get more out of life?
- What if I were authorized to reach my true potential and live a full life, the life I've always imagined?
- What if I were meant to win at the game of life?
- What do you think? Do you want to stay fired, stuck, complacent, uninspired, lackluster, being what everyone else wants or needs you to be?

Or do you want to claim your destiny and search for the right coach, find the right coach, and hire the right coach to help build the life you've always known you were meant to have? The coach that will help you find the direction of your dreams and give you the tools you need to achieve your own fulfillment?

Good news! You can do this! It is possible. There's a coach out there who will show you the practical steps to take to realize the power that already exists within you and give license and consent to its tangible emergence.

## Chapter Two

# THE RIGHT SUPPORT

Before we go any further, push your reset buttons. Then ask yourself, "What do I need to achieve my full potential?"

A lot of things will come to mind. For now, in this moment, focus on this one answer to your question: a coach. A life coach. Someone who is only successful if you are successful.

This someone needs to point out the things you are doing that further your growth and the things you are doing to stifle it. You need someone who can support and guide you, cheer you on, and help you understand yourself at the deepest level. You need someone to get you out of your rut and up to higher ground.

Don't misunderstand. All the other things that entered your mind when you asked yourself the question are important and relevant. There is absolutely nothing wrong with having a fulfilling relationship. There is nothing bad about having friends and family who care about you. These aren't things you need to give up.

The difference is it is time to pay special attention to whether you are actually looking for support and encouragement from relationships that may not be in your best interest, which may even be damaging your self-confidence or limiting your vision.

Right now is the right time to recognize the difference between someone who can make you stronger and help you grow, or someone who is no longer serving your higher good. You need to be willing to walk away from what is holding you back and be willing to find out what moves you forward.

Before my journey with life coaches began, my life had been a fairly unremarkable series of both successes and failures. I lived what people might refer to as a "normal" life.

I was brought up in a loving household that seemed to function about the same as everybody else's. We celebrated, quarreled, loved each other fiercely one minute and drove each other wild the next. Life carried on with the usual ebbs and flows of a typical family. My mother was a corporate nurse, and my dad was an engineer. Both worked for large corporations and were handsomely reimbursed for their labor, a detail that did not go unnoticed by our neighbors.

But my parents differed from Jack and Jill's parents in that, as well as having their day jobs, they were also ministers who played an active role in the Christian church

I grew up in, and both served on the priesthood. So, religion was a big part of my upbringing.

Jesus was a regular topic in our dinner table conversation, and he was always praised, whether or not you were following his word. Taboo topics such as cussing, drinking, smoking, and having sex were never discussed, nor were they tolerated.

So, I learned by watching my siblings: two older sisters and an older brother. They were 9, 10, and 11 years my seniors, with my brother being closest to me in age. Their personalities were as diverse as they were big. Being the youngest, I either sat still and watched the chaos ensue, or I yelled, cried, kicked, and screamed to get attention. I became an attention seeker.

Growing up in this kind of household was very confusing for a child like me. I was hypersensitive from the beginning, and I hung on to every word my siblings and parents uttered. I don't think they realized just how much they influenced my thinking. I always took them at their word.

One day, my brother said it was going to rain. I asked how he knew. He said, "It's written in the sky, can't you see it?" So, taking him at his word, I looked up at the sky and was bewildered when I didn't see anything written in the clouds.

Then I started learning things on my own, sometimes the easy way and sometimes the hard way. One of the most indelible lessons I learned growing up was how *not* to be. The underlying message I heard was:

"Don't be yourself."

"Why?"

"Because the neighbors will notice. You don't want to stand out, you want to fit in."

This premise carried me into my adult life. *Don't be me! Pretend to be someone I'm not so I can fit in.*

I am not saying this is what anyone intended for me to learn, but it is the truth of what I did learn. I learned how to fit in, how to drink like the rest of them, pray like the rest of them, go to work like the rest of them. I got married and had three children and a good job as a physical therapist. We lived in an affluent neighborhood with lovely neighbors, a beautiful house, and good cars. I had everything I had ever dreamed of, or so it seemed.

I looked and acted happy on the outside, but an ever-present void lingered on the inside.

I tried to figure out what was "wrong" with me. I went to doctors and therapists, and I participated in a variety of self-help and 12-step programs. I read and reread all the books Oprah recommended, got involved in church, and even ran a marathon! I was determined to backfill my emptiness and conquer the pursuit of happiness, no matter what.

However, I didn't know who I was or what I truly wanted. Inevitably, I found myself divorced, bankrupt, and completely lost. I lost my job of 14 years, my marriage, and partial custody of my children. I was more than just financially bankrupt—I was broken. I went from having it all to having nothing.

After the divorce, I had to learn some hard things, like how to rely on myself. I had to learn to live on my own for the first time in my life. I had to learn who I was and what I wanted. That's when I discovered I really had no clue how to live without someone next to me. My codependent patterns were so deeply engrained that I was in a whirlwind in my brain, desperately seeking a new identity.

And that is what led me to a very dark period. I was fortunate that this dark time lasted only a few months, but I packed more darkness in those few months than most would pack into several years.

There's a saying that only through the darkness can one come to see the light. At that point, my life was pitch black. Despite the saying, I personally do not believe that everyone has to go through a dark time in order to experience the light; however, I did. And this is my story, which I am sharing in the hope that it will save you and others the heartache I went through.

Actually, I have always looked for the light. I've even been called a light seeker. I see the light in others almost immediately. I have an uncanny ability to recognize people's strengths and envision their path, yet when it came to me, I couldn't pinpoint my strengths and lingered too long on my weaknesses.

This is typical of human beings. Until we gain enough of the right kind of awareness, we are quick to point out other people's flaws yet fail to see our own, or we sing others' praises while feeling inferior ourselves.

This is why having someone help you raise your awareness is so vitally important. That's what coaches and mentors provide, and everyone needs them. Even the best of the best had or have mentors and coaches. Ralph Waldo Emerson mentored Henry David Thoreau, then after Thoreau put Emerson's words into action, he mentored Emerson. Mother Teresa revered her mentor Father Michael van der Peet. Oprah Winfrey pays tribute to her mentor Maya Angelou by saying, "She was there for me always, guiding me through some of the most important years of my life. Mentors are important, and I don't think anybody makes it in the world without some form of mentorship."

Heed those words! A life coach can make all the difference in your life! Each of us has the opportunity to stand on the shoulders of giants. It's time to look to those who have paved the road you walk, listen to what they have learned, and apply their wisdom to your own growth.

My mentor, Bob Proctor, has mentored and coached countless people, all because he is passionate about passing on to others what Earl Nightingale passed on to him. That is how brilliant beginnings are birthed: when one enlightened human being shares what worked for them with another, they bring the other into their glory or light. As the hymn

"Amazing Grace" says, "I once was lost, but now am found, was blind, but now I see."

The journey toward your fulfillment is not on a path you walk alone. You need a guide! It is not just about achieving your goals (although this will be one of the many benefits). It is about shifting your perception of the world and of yourself to see the bigger picture. This enhanced perception and awareness allow you to be *all* you can be.

Follow along, and you'll see what I mean.

Chapter Three

# DITCH THE BOYFRIEND

Before I dive into exactly what a life coach can do for you, I want to explain why it is important to figuratively ditch the boyfriend.

*Disclaimer:* I am not recommending you abandon healthy relationships. Please read on.

When I was growing up, I always dreamed of marrying the right guy and living happily ever after. I suppose it was impressed upon me that having a husband and family was my only ticket to happiness and fulfillment.

I am not 100 percent sure why I believed this. Using my mom and dad as a model for this theory, I certainly would not have come to this conclusion. Although they had a successful marriage in the end, they did not emanate love and compassion for one another when I was younger. Their fights were frequent and destructive, with their mutually explosive tempers leaving a backlash of debris all around them. Slamming doors, throwing things, yelling, and threatening divorce were regular occurrences. I don't mean this to be disrespectful to my parents at all (especially my mother who is still living), but it is how I remember their relationship growing up.

I also remember escaping to my bedroom at a very young age and playing house with my baby dolls and stuffed animals. My game always involved a perfect family with me as the nurturer of my children and animals. Through this innocently childish, escapist role play, my yearning to have my perfect dream family grew stronger day by day.

I was eventually old enough to date and always felt I picked wisely. In fact, I would often say to myself how proud I was of being a good "picker," meaning I picked "good guys."

Looking back, almost all my relationships were, to some degree, toxic. I now realize that the common denominator was—you guessed it—the one and only me.

Although I really enjoyed others' company and love, they were a kind of filler for the emptiness and unease within me. There were times when I would assume the role of manipulator and try to control their behavior through a myriad of dysfunctional ways, in order to try to fill this need. After all, this is what I had learned growing up. I had learned not to be myself, but to fit in at all costs. Which, in turn, left me feeling very empty and confused, not to mention unable to be alone. The relationships I sought out were a temporary calm for the constant storm inside.

I mean, I knew what I did *not* want a relationship to look like. *I* would not have the relationship my parents did.

*I* would not have the problems they had, and *I* most certainly would not have the family they had.

I would do things differently and live the life of my dreams.

As you know by now, things didn't go quite as planned.

What actually happened is that I brought learned behaviors and relationship habits into my marriage. As a parent, I did some things better than my parents and some things worse. I did not earn the parent of the year award *ever*, but I certainly tried to be the best mom I could be. But the truth is, I ended up replicating the types of relationships I tried so desperately to avoid.

After the divorce, I vowed my life would be different. *If* I dated, I would find the perfect man and have the perfect relationship. I did not know that my lack of awareness about myself would only keep me in the same cycle that many of us grow up with—the belief that we will be happy when we get married and have children or do other external things differently. I was not taught to seek happiness within myself, but instead, to look outward for it. Happiness depended on circumstances, choice of partner, jobs, money, and material possessions. Again, all outside myself. Outside my control.

No wonder society is riddled with addictions of all kinds. The 12-step program houses millions (this number continues to grow) of people with over 60 kinds of addictions who come together with a common interest—to heal their lives. At the heart of all these addictions is that fundamentally false and misleading premise that our happiness resides in someone or something outside ourselves.

This is proof that we did not receive and are not instilling in our children the belief that everything they need to succeed they hold within themselves. This is the truth that we need to embrace and impart.

I believe one way to help the world is to begin helping ourselves. I'm not talking about being selfish or narcissistic or self-centered. I mean loving ourselves exactly as we are right now by making a commitment to take care of ourselves and stop turning to other people or things for fulfillment. To leave the destructive relationship and spend time with ourselves, learning how to be our own best friend and confidante. The degree to which we are comfortable with ourselves is measured by how content we feel in the presence of our own company. This is where the healing has to begin.

Our society is full of deeply codependent people who cannot spend time alone. We are constantly seeking the approval of others instead of learning how to be comfortable and confident in our own skin. When isolation was imposed during the COVID-19 pandemic, many people were on their own, some for the first time. Extroverts had a difficult time, but introverts struggled as well. Our society is built on interactive social platforms, and a great deal of mental anguish came out during the pandemic because of our limited ability to actually *be* with others.

Our need for approval outside ourselves, particularly among women, is a magnet for abusive relationships. Abusers are adept at sensing vulnerability as early as the initial meeting. They impose their diseased thinking onto this vulnerable person, who perceives it as attention and love. In reality, it can be truly soul crushing. A worthy partner will not exploit neediness but allow their loved one to stand on their own while providing support and empathy.

Increasing numbers of people are waking up to the importance of leaving destructive, codependent relationships and learning to become their own best friends. They are realizing their strength and relying on it to create their best life.

It is a beautiful thing to see a woman go from being in a relationship that is sucking the life out of her to truly doing what it takes to stand on her own. The empowered and enlightened woman can establish her own life and her own rhythm before inviting anyone else to become part of her life. She is developing strong female friendships and busy creating the life of her dreams. This became and is *my life*!

If this sounds like something you would like, and you have not taken the time to be by yourself, for yourself, alone, then prepare for the biggest change in your life. It is time to get real with yourself, establish some boundaries, and leave your toxic BS behind.

It is hard work, but you can do it, because the answer to winning in your life is not finding yourself in a relationship. It is finding yourself within yourself. Searching for your authentic power—or wholeness—in another person is doomed to failure and heartbreak.

If you are struggling to leave an emotionally or physically abusive relationship, I want you to make a promise to yourself today to get the help you need. In my experience, you cannot recover from abuse without support. (Turn to Appendix A: Barbara's Favorite Resources right now and try out one of the links.)

If you are a person that is sick and tired of the bullshit involved in dating and falling into a relationship with mediocre people, there is a solution.

Stop!

Next, take three big steps.

**Step one:** start dating yourself! Make a commitment to be with and for yourself. You attract what you seek. But if your life is not what you want it to be, it isn't because someone else is sabotaging it. It is because *you* are sabotaging your life.

This is *your* life, and only you have the power to change it. No matter what your current situation is right now, you can and will win at this life you have been given, but only *if* you start fresh now and never give up!

Furthermore, if you are currently not where you want to be in life or are not being the whole person you know you are capable of being, you are—in essence—putting out a lot of bullshit vibes. And those vibes are attracting some greater bullshit into your life. As the saying goes, "Your vibe attracts your tribe." And so it is.

To get rid of the bullshit in your life, you have to get rid of the dysfunctional beliefs and destructive behaviors. The best way to do this is to spend time alone.

**Step two:** get the right kind of support to transform yourself and your life. You will find no better support than a life coach to move your life in the direction you want it to go. So, ditch the boyfriend, girlfriend, or whatever is holding you back, and use the tools in this book to get a life coach.

Once you've spent time alone, then started working with a life coach, the next step is a natural.

**Step three:** start now, start new, start being the best possible you in the universe.

Chapter Four

# LIFE COACHING 101

Life coaching is absolutely booming right now, a trend I am very excited about. LifeCoach.com states: "If there is a gap between where you are now and where you want to be, then there is room for life coaching." This pretty much sums up the whole human race, so everyone could use a life coach.

I will go a step further and say that not only could everyone use a life coach, but also that everyone actually *needs* one.

A relationship with a life coach is unlike any other relationship we've had or will have. It is like having a therapist, consultant, mentor, cheerleader, and friend all bottled up in one person.

This bond may be similar to the kind of relationship you have with a therapist in that you are seeking guidance to overcome obstacles in your life. A good therapist enables their clients to identify dysfunctional patterns of behavior and develop new ones. I am not saying give up therapy. What I am saying is there are fundamental differences between a therapist and a life coach.

Many forms of therapy focus on healing the past by taking you back through what has happened. Life coaching focuses on how to do things differently now and in the future. It opens your mind so you can gain awareness. It makes you better equipped to reframe old wounds while also building new behaviors for future fulfillment.

A business consultant can guide you in a decision-making process to move forward professionally. A life coach will help you to see what is holding you back, what is working well for you, and how to apply what you learn to grow and develop skills to meet your life goals.

A life coach will require that you take an inventory of yourself, much as you would before making a change in your business.

Life coaches are skilled at identifying your strengths and guiding you in the direction that best fits *you* and *your* dreams.

The relationship between you and a life coach definitely mimics mentoring, which is why it is crucial you choose a life coach that has accomplished some of the things you aspire to or who has unique ideas that support your goals. A mentor can be anybody who serves as a teacher or guide. A typical example of a mentoring relationship would be a senior company employee who takes a new or less experienced employee under their wing and shows them how to work in the most effective manner. In this way, your coach is indeed your mentor.

Most coaches have been through a coaching experience themselves, and for many of them, myself included, that experience was the catalyst for the passion they feel for this role. It's how they know what works and what doesn't. Also, since they are winning at the game of life, they are going to show you how to win as well!

Your life coach is also your personal cheerleader and is as invested in your journey as you are. Your success is their success. They are going to absolutely let you know when you are doing things well, and you'd better believe they'll let you know when you are slipping back into old habits that don't serve you. You can expect a lot of high fives and jumping up and down, whether figuratively or literally, throughout this journey, but you can expect some well-meaning and honest butt-kicking, too. Your life coach will not only tell you when you're off track but will use specific tactics to get you back on track. They will be your loudest voice of encouragement until they get you to truly see and believe that the tactics they are teaching you are working, by which time you will have become your own best cheerleader.

One of the most alluring and unique aspects of this professional relationship is that the bond you create allows you to be seen, heard, understood, and honored— no matter where you have been, what you have done, or what you do. It is certainly one of the most nonjudgmental relationships I have had in my life. This is what makes the relationship feel like more than just business or therapy.

It allows you to explore your ability to trust someone else in a truly unique way.

You will be stretched in ways you've never imagined, growing far beyond your perceived capabilities. You will be shown the infinite possibilities that exist within you and how to easily bring them to life.

In this way a life coach is your absolute best tool to living your best life. But it's so much more. Imagine a world where everyone is striving to be their best self. I believe we would live in a changed world. That's why I believe life coaching is what the whole world needs.

Even if you don't buy into the theory that our world would change if each individual were living their most fulfilled and productive life, you can certainly buy into the notion that having a life coach will change your world. Google it—you will see. Life coaching has time and time again brought people to levels they never dreamed possible. Life coaches will help you work through your issues, decide your next move, see your strengths, show you how to be the best version of yourself, inspire and encourage you, and love you as only they can through it all. You will be empowered and unstoppable!

Whatever your goals—no matter how simple or complex—your life coach will have your back until your achieve them, and then be with you as you move beyond into even greater achievements. Having a life coach is for everyone. Having a life coach is for you!

It's time to ask yourself, what is the one dream you keep holding on to?

Got an answer? Great. Now, find a life coach and make that dream a reality! Given that there are several million people in the world who claim to be life coaches, keep reading to learn how to find one with those key qualities for your best match.

Chapter Five

# MY JOURNEY

Before I began my journey with a life coach, there were signs that started presenting themselves to me. The signs that I received were universal. They came more often and grew more obvious, so that by the time I began working with a life coach, I was primed and ready to move forward with my goals.

I will also point out what happened when I made the commitment to begin so that you can see how quickly and easily things can turn around. This narrative will also be a good segue to the next chapter where I describe the key elements of an outstanding life coach.

For now, let's go back to where we left off in my life story.

I was divorced, had partial custody of my children, and was attempting to make adjustments that demanded more than I possessed.

Divorce is traumatic. You can't get around it. It just is. With children in the mix, it can be downright heartbreaking.

In the first few months after the divorce, I was blissfully unaware of how much pain I was in. I had my own apartment for the first time ever where the children came for half of each week. I missed them like crazy when they were gone, but I was enjoying dating and doing things on my own. I was finding my way through the pain and having a little fun. I recognized early on in the divorce process that it was meant to be, and that I needed to be divorced to find myself.

During this earth-shattering shift my life was taking, there were little signs that kept giving me hope. There were physical signs that I took as signs from the universe that I was on the right path. The first physical sign was the double rainbow that appeared in the sky as I was moving into my new apartment. After that, people began showing up in my life who I believe were showing me the way to embrace my changes.

One day, when I was outside my new apartment tending to my little front garden, a woman walked by with her dogs.

"Your garden is lovely," she said. "I can see your happiness reflected in it. The more beautiful the garden, the happier the individual tending it."

I certainly didn't feel like the happiest person, but I was learning to be happy. I had also learned to wear masks very well and pretend to be happy when I wasn't. That day I was feeling particularly lonely, so I put the mask on and politely thanked her. We began a conversation that lasted more than an hour.

Her name was Barbara, too. Odd coincidence. She was so happy and open that I wanted to know more about her, so I kept asking questions.

She spoke of her life before her awareness of who she really was, transitioning later into tales of her grand life now—the life of her dreams. As she spoke, I felt myself yearning for that sense of fulfillment.

In the end, she attributed her growth to her divorce and soul searching. The book that changed the trajectory of her life was *Ask and It Is Given* by Esther and Jerry Hicks.

"That's funny," I said. "I have that book in my basement. I started reading it, but it was a little too weird for me."

It was weird. I purchased the book five to seven years prior and had begun reading it. The preface was about an out-of-body experience that Esther had when meditating. She began receiving information from an entity called Abraham. Weird. Period. Not for me. Period.

I didn't mention in detail how I had initially felt about the book to my new friend Barbara. I kept my commentary to myself.

The final thing she left me with was: "I learned all about Esther and the law of attraction through my life coach, and I wouldn't trade the experience for the world."

We parted ways, sharing our mutual delight in meeting each other and feeling a connection. I vowed that day that I would read that book. And I did.

But I was sure I would not need a life coach. I could figure this game out myself. How hard could it be?

As I read Esther's words, I began digesting the law of attraction. "You bring about what you think about" was the key idea. I didn't pursue it intently at first. I just read it, became familiar with the idea, and slowly came to believe wholeheartedly in that premise.

My main purpose at this time was to fill my lonely, broken heart. Date after date and a few men later, I found myself more isolated than ever before. I could write a whole book on the topic of divorce rebound and why not to date immediately following, but I will save that saga for another time. Let's just say I was completely unaware of my issues and, again, I kept looking for love in all the wrong places.

I didn't get the message the first time, so another messenger was sent.

While in Walgreens one day, I bumped into an old friend. She wasn't one of the neighborhood friends who didn't know how to address me or approach me since I was now divorced. She wasn't one of the parents of my children's friends. She wasn't one of my friends who wondered why I left my job. She was a woman I had met some time ago through mutual friends. We weren't close—we'd lost touch over the years, but we were more than acquaintances. I'd seen her face pop up on Facebook. She looked happy. But everyone looks happy on Facebook.

She told me she would like to get together sometime, and I agreed aloud while thinking, "She's not my kind of people." But she persisted, and after a few months, we got together.

She told me she had been in a codependent cyclone from hell but was now living the most joyous and favorable life she could imagine. What were her secrets? The law of attraction and, you guessed it, her amazing life coach!

This time, when I heard this phenomenal story, I didn't cringe. Instead, I felt comforted, like someone had enveloped my freezing cold body with a freshly warmed blanket, welcoming me home.

That woman is now a dear friend of mine. She tells me today she persisted because she was led to, that she knew she needed to reach me. In my darkest hours, she was there with a phone call or a text to cheer me up. Daily messages and weekly phone calls led to me gaining traction on my own and leaving the search for a man in the dust.

I shifted my focus to searching for my place in this Great Big World and how to start winning at life! However, the game turned out to be trickier than I had anticipated. One day I would be winning big and finding my way and then the next, I would be losing again. I'd get a grip on it again, just to have it seized away. I didn't have a name for it then but now I call it the dance of the addicted. It was the push and pull of unhealthy behaviors that had permeated my life. I just couldn't let them go.

But the signs kept coming, from double rainbows to people entering my life and lifting me up to a higher level of conscious living. These were people I couldn't ignore, as much as I tried. The final sign was being stuck in a cycle of behavior that was causing pain, and this time I was aware the cycle was of my own doing. It also became obvious that

I couldn't end the cycle and find the life that I so desperately wanted—without help. So, when my dear friend suggested I see her life coach, I did. I was ready. I connected with my new lease on life—this life coach—on a weekly basis.

In *weeks*, I was able to see my life from a higher perspective than ever before. I became quickly and powerfully aware of the reasons for my unhealthy patterns of behavior, patterns that would keep leading me back to the path I was trying so desperately to avoid.

Within three months, I was living a happier and more joyous life than I had ever lived before. As a child I dreamed of a grand life for myself, and these dreams were finally being reawakened. The part of me that reawakened was the part that knew what I wanted and that I had it in me to achieve my goals. The words and techniques the life coach was using at that time spoke to a deeper part of me, a part that had been closed and dormant but was finally open and permitted to take on the world, heart, and soul!

Over those three months, I became completely comfortable in my own skin. I healed familial relationships. I discovered I was not only capable of but actually enjoyed being alone. Deep, secure female friendships I had always wanted were present in my life. I found a new job with a $30,000-plus increase in pay. My self-confidence was through the roof, and I had begun trusting my intuition for the first time in my life. I was winning.

I uncovered a profound understanding that I had always had it in me to live the life I wanted. What I lacked was the guidance I needed to help me navigate *my* life's path.

Sound exciting? Wait, there's more.

Chapter Six

# KICK-ASS LIFE COACH QUALITIES

You may be wondering at this point what I did to implement so much change and become prosperous is such a short time. However, my mission in writing this book is not to tell you what I did specifically. That is because each person must do different things—take their own path, if you will—in order to reach their goals. What worked for me may not work for you and vice versa. But since this is about sharing the secret to unlocking your power, or inner guidance, to achieve all you wish to have in your life, I'll repeat, the secret is a life coach! Not just any life coach. The right life coach for your life.

Not all life coaches are created equal. Shop around, and shop carefully, as you would for anything of value. Life coaches may have similar skills, but they do not all have equal information, and it is the *information* that will change your life. It is the information that they pass on to you that will allow you to become your own powerful center and produce the results you desire in any area of your life.

In the previous chapter, I shared how I had connected with a life coach and that as a result of this connection I made dramatic improvements in my life within three months. In this chapter, I am going to share the top attributes of a quality life coach and the importance of a life coaching program.

When I began working with my first life coach, the one I spoke of in the last chapter, my life shifted quickly. This success came from dedication and effort. Make no mistake, I was 100 percent committed to doing whatever my life coach told me to do and do it to the best of my ability. I was done taking a half-assed approach to life. I was ready for true change.

I worked diligently on my homework assignments, and as I did this, I began to form questions that my life coach couldn't answer. She had given me a new lease on life and inspired me to follow my own guidance, but I started feeling unsettled. It wasn't clear to me what I was looking for at the time, but I knew I craved more information.

Then I decided to look for someone who might be more aligned with my thinking and business aspirations. Throughout that process, I was consuming information and relying on my intuition more every day.

I had also begun doing some things that brought positive energy into my life, such as writing a blog. I named the blog *In My Halo*. It was about my path to finding my best self. One thing led to another, and I ended up using Instagram as a mini daily blog. (You can still see these posts on my current Instagram page: @barbarajoycelive.)

I fell in love with the positive vibes on Instagram and was posting twice a day. I engaged a bit with other people who were doing the same—sharing energy and lifting each other up. And that is how I met my next life coach.

If you had told me that I would find a life coach online and pay good money to start working with him, I would have told you that you were absolutely bonkers! Today, I acknowledge it is one of the best investments I have ever made.

Then the next change hit. My intuition and understanding of the higher aptitudes of my mind were still not fully formed, and it took some time before I was able to make a firm commitment to find yet another new life coach.

I really wanted to move forward in my life, and I needed the next person I worked with to be the right fit so I would get the results I sought. I interviewed three life coaches. I was also meditating and tuning in to my inner guidance about what I wanted. The more I tuned in to myself, the less I listened to other people's opinions.

The combination of trusting myself and providence (in this case, meeting the right life coach) was a phenomenal experience. The outcome, the feeling of certainty was so profound, I didn't question it. Despite my firm belief in my decision, I had one tiny hurdle standing in my way. I still couldn't see how I would be able to afford it.

I decided to make an intention in writing that I wanted to work with this life coach. I wanted it so badly, and it became clearer with each day, although my patience was tested. Then I found the money to pay for his services. I messaged him, "I'm ready!" I paid him that day and began working with him five days later.

I worked with this life coach for the next seven months. The information he shared was exactly what I had been craving. There was one particular reading I did that made me weep because I knew I had truly started to uncover the secrets I had yearned to uncover for so long. That reading was Geneviève Behrend's book *Your Invisible Power*.

I thought I had found the coach that I would be learning from for the rest of my life, but I was still thirsty for more. With gratitude, we parted ways, and I continued to seek out the knowledge I yearned for on my own.

Then I happened upon Bob Proctor's Paradigm Shift program. I purchased it online and began livestreaming. The more I listened, the further my jaw dropped. All the information I had spent months learning with my last life coach was presented to me over a weekend by Bob Proctor.

As is most often the case, one thing led to another. I started teaching the material I was taught through the Proctor Gallagher Institute. Through this work and this company, I found the most amazing group of inspirational leaders from all over the world, working together for one common purpose: to help individuals be their best selves and live as we are designed to live.

After working with the institute, I knew I wanted to develop my own program that combined the spiritual principles of the 12-step program with the laws of creation I learned with Bob Proctor. Today, my program can provide a life-altering structure for those who align with it. You can find my program here: www.barbarajoyce.com/radicalrising

I am very excited and humbled to be fully supported as I step into my true purpose in life. I am especially passionate about working with women to help them create quantum leaps in their income and life choices by getting rid of the bullshit and taking back their power! This is where my journey and my heart are today. I believe firmly in the information I teach. I know there are other life coaches out there teaching great material as well. It's all about finding the best fit.

Because I believe so strongly in life coaching, I want to make it as straightforward as possible for you to find *your* qualified life coach.[1] Here's the list:

---

[1] The most comprehensive information I found was on Evercoach by Mindvalley (https://www.evercoach.com). The 20 general attributes as identified by Evercoach are essential to any life coach. If you get any inkling these traits are not present in someone you have hired, or are thinking of hiring, run in the other direction. In the article, Evercoach breaks down each characteristic with a brief description. (You can check out their article at: https://www.evercoach.com/blog/20-born-to-coach-personality-traits-all-great-coaches-share)

## The Top 20 General Life Coach Attributes

1. Compassionate
2. Supportive
3. Learning machine
4. Innovative
5. Humble
6. Awesome listener
7. Curious
8. Grateful
9. Excellent communicator
10. Positive
11. Visionary
12. Courageous
13. Observant
14. Focused
15. Dedicated
16. Honest
17. Professional
18. Trustworthy
19. Modeling
20. Sincere

Your life coach should definitely be compassionate, supportive, grateful, and positive. They should be someone who shows that they care and are there to help you. They should demonstrate respect for the time and money you are choosing to spend with them. And they should always present themselves and their ideas with a positive and empowering demeanor. This demeanor will make you want to jump up off the couch and dig into working with them.

Curious, observant, great listener, excellent communicator, courageous, and humble may also seem like no-brainer traits to have in your life coach; however, don't overlook them! These six traits tend to go hand in hand. Your coach needs to demonstrate a genuine curiosity about you by listening to what you are telling them and observing the things you aren't telling them. They should communicate their findings in a way that is both courageous and humble. Courage is a trait that comes from telling you some things you may not want to hear, or hard truths. And humility comes from communicating information and observations in a way that is neither patronizing nor arrogant. After all, nobody likes a know-it-all. The humble coach speaks to you in a manner that allows you to make the discovery (mostly) yourself.

You need someone on your team who is focused, dedicated, professional, honest, trustworthy, and sincere. Their commitment to the purpose they play in your life is absolutely necessary! Their ability to stay focused keeps you focused as well, and you should sense this from early on. Professionalism is a must. This is a unique relationship, and at times you may feel that your life coach is one of your best friends. It is a truly wonderful part of the life coach's role, but the line of professionalism should never be crossed. They will give you pertinent information about their life and their journey, but they will not dump their issues on you. A professional life coach will never discuss other clients in specific terms. They will be honest in all their efforts with you and trustworthy, making you feel extremely safe. A life coach will want the best for you.

Last but definitely not least, these are the most important traits of all: a life coach must be a learning machine, innovative, visionary, and worthy of modeling. These are the aspects that set a life-changing coach apart from a mediocre one. The person needs to be light years ahead of you in terms of knowledge, but they should also demonstrate a continued eagerness for learning and growing. This capacity and yearning for knowledge will help you immensely as your relationship with your life coach evolves and transforms. If they are not actively seeking more knowledge, run, don't walk, the other way. I say this because they are going to be teaching you what they know about how to win, and if they aren't themselves growing, you will inevitably outgrow them.

The best life coaches are learning all the time. It is what makes them great as they innovate new ways of working with you and help you develop your skills. This information not only feeds their vision for themselves and their future, but also allows them to envision new possibilities for you to explore that can push you beyond your comfort zone. By their example, they are giving you a blueprint for how you can achieve your goals. Modeling is used in cognitive behavioral therapy to change the responses of the client. It is actually a very important phenomenon that makes life coaches one of the best mediums for change in a person's life.

I could go into deep detail about modeling, but for the purpose of this book, all you need to know is to have a coach that has attributes that you want to see in yourself.

Now that you know the general attributes, let's look at the four critical, kick-ass attributes. Remember, if you are going to hire someone to change your life, they need to have something extra—the X factor! That someone is a person of strong integrity who is privy to the kind of information that will propel you to unprecedented success in any area of your life.

You are investing in yourself, and you want to make sure you are choosing wisely. Furthermore, if you want your dreams to come true, you are going to need someone extra special by your side—a kick-ass life coach (who will propel you to unparalleled success). [2]Now that you know the general attributes, let's look at the four critical, kick-ass attributes

---

[2] I have included a Life Coach Interview Checklist in Appendix B. I recommend you interview three coaches before deciding on one. Make sure they get 100 percent right.

## Top Four Qualities of an Absolutely Kick-Ass Life Coach

### 1. A Life Coach Who Uses a Program with a Proven Track Record of Results

There are two reasons I consider this item to be the top priority: time and energy.

Time is important because this work requires full commitment. With a well-organized program in place, you lock in for a designated period of time, such as 6, 12, or 18 months. The program itself is defined by its duration. Once time and your commitment are firm and once you are dedicated to diving into the materials, you are ready to dig deeper within yourself to expand your abilities. Moreover, because you know there is a deadline, the chances of you copping out are slim. This time factor also keeps your life coach committed to and focused on you for a dedicated period of time.

This dynamic creates a momentum of its own, which will then lend itself to a steady stream of energy, the second important factor in a program. The energy someone brings to any situation determines its transformative power. It is no different in this relationship. The energy expended will determine the change. When you combine condensed time and focused energy, the transformation takes on a life of its own. Change is not only inevitable but also quick, and the effects of this change will alter the course of your life.

This may seem like a grand promise, but it is actually natural. Time and energy play a vital role in creating momentum in countless aspects of our lives. It is the same principle with life coaching. Think of it in terms of a work deadline. Let's say you have been assigned a project you estimate will only take you a week to finish, but you've been given a month. It's highly likely that the amount of energy you initially bring to the program will be low. Plus, you are likely to procrastinate, only gaining energy as you approach the deadline. So now... imagine you were given only a week to complete this same project, and you believed it would take you the full week to complete it. You would put all your energy into the project from the onset, ensuring better results. That's how it is with a proven program: you bring all your energy to the table in the time allotted.

This energy is generated not only by you, but also by your life coach and the program itself, making it analogous to a three-stranded rope versus a two-stranded rope. A two-stranded rope is much weaker than a three-stranded rope. Without a program in place, you only have a two-stranded rope: you and your life coach. The three-stranded rope is much stronger and yields far superior results. The first strand is the life coach, the second strand is you, and the third strand is the program itself.

Go for the coach with a program to maximize time and energy so you can make your life coaching experience a success! The program must provide structure and support. Unless you have those things, there is an increased potential for disorganized thinking. The go-with-the-flow mentality can lead to endless work without a true goal or destination and could go on indefinitely. If the goal is just to feel better, you can choose *any* life coach. But to accomplish that dream you originally thought was impossible, there has to be a solid combination of information and approaches that have been tested and proven to deliver results.

Look for a well-structured program to yield the best outcomes. Whether the program is the life coach's own creation or that of a company, the program must demonstrate that participants grow exponentially and achieve the goals they set. Don't be shy to ask for word-of-mouth referrals from previous clients. If you were hiring a new employee for a company, you would speak with previous employers, right? You should do the same before hiring a life coach.

Once you have looked at the track record of the clients, go a step further. Most businesses will have glowing testimonials. Go beyond these straight to the source: the coach. Why? Because the results of an effective program should be reflected in the coach's own life. The right coach with the right program will have successful results from their students and model it in their own life. You want to work with someone who will help you win in life, make money, improve, feel better, be better. They cannot do that if they don't have their own life together.

Again, to make sure you are embarking on a win-win situation, research the program, the outcomes of clients, and the life of the life coach.

## 2. A Life Coach Who Has Keen Intuition

This remarkable trait is one you should actively seek out in your life coach. These words—keen intuition—are not chosen lightly. First, let's take a look at the meaning of the word intuition. Intuition is a function of the mind that circumvents the need for conscious reasoning. It is what we call our gut instinct. In my experience, we are not readily encouraged to use our intuition. In fact, we are taught that decisions should be made using logic. It was not until I began working with life coaches that I realized the importance of strengthening and using this invaluable faculty. Remember, this is your inner voice, and like any instrument, it requires ongoing practice to use it and master it.

I say *remember* because it is my belief that we are all born with equal intuitive abilities at birth that, in most of us, are strongest when we are young. Of course, how strong or acute our instincts remain is dependent on many factors. We all have societal programming that either encourages or discourages our use of this innate sense, which naturally, leads to differing abilities. That said, like any muscle, intuition can be reconditioned through training and practice.

When looking for a life coach, it is best to look for one that exercises their intuition in how they teach and learn. It needs to be keen, or finely sharpened, through practice and application, honed, tuned for a purpose. Keen intuition is a useful tool that quality coaches employ. They are able to see you in a way that no one else can. In order to nudge you in a certain direction, their instincts need to be acute. Keen intuition is invaluable.

### 3. A Life Coach Who Can Connect with You

It is vitally important that the life coach connects deeply with you. Let me give you an example of what this looked like in my life.

When I was looking for a life coach that was more aligned with my aspirations for a career change, I found one on Instagram. I started following him and felt a connection with the words on his posts. Once I interviewed with him, I knew he had the information I was looking for. The words and ideas he expressed rang true deep in my soul. I felt a tug in my heart I could not ignore.

My interview with this life coach lasted a few hours. During this time, I saw in broad terms why I had been unable to figure out this game of life—a rude but welcome awakening. I was not only standing in my own way— I didn't know how to get out of my way. I needed assistance to go the direction I wanted to go.

After this inspiring interview, I was driving and listening to an episode of *Oprah's SuperSoul Conversations* with Jack Canfield called "Fulfilling Your Soul's Purpose." Jack Canfield, in case you are not familiar with him, built the largest publishing empire in history with Mark Victor

Hansen. In this particular podcast episode, Jack talked about finding your soul's purpose. When I heard what he said, I got chills up and down my spine. In fact, he said several things in that episode that resonated profoundly with me.

The first thing Jack stated was, "You won't be allowed to have the dream if you don't have the ability to achieve it." I had lots of dreams and aspirations. Was he saying I could achieve them all?

The second thing Jack said was, "Joy is your guidance system." He talked about how he no longer received joy from writing *Chicken Soup for the Soul*, that he needed to move on to something different. I related to this on many levels. I had not felt joy in my work as a physical therapist for years. Was he suggesting that I needed a change?

The final point that spoke instantly to me was, "You can't miss your soul's purpose. It will call to you until you can't avoid it." This hit home, and it hit hard. It was exactly how I felt during this interview. I felt like my thoughts and feelings were on another dimension entirely.

I was on the verge. I sensed my soul's purpose calling me, but it was elusive. I wanted to write but I didn't know what to write. I wanted to teach but I didn't know what I wanted to teach. I wanted to help people live healthy and happy lives, but how would I do that? I wanted to give more to the world, help people, and live the life of my dreams, but I was clueless as to how to go about that.

I did know was there was a yearning in me to be more. I could not put my finger on what "more" was, or how to unleash that potential, but after talking with this life coach, I felt we had connected. When he spoke about the importance of finding purpose and how that will guide and shape life, I felt like I'd found the missing pieces of my puzzle.

Believe me, when you find that, you will know!

By finding a life coach that can connect with you deeply, you will unlock what has been waiting to be released your whole life. You will recognize that you have found the right fit because it will be confirmed by your own intuition.

Your intuition is that little instinctual voice inside your head that tells you how you feel about something. It doesn't care much for logic or rationale, nor does it ask why or how. It just is and it knows. And, as I said earlier, when you find the right life coach, you will know. It may hit you as a sudden epiphany or as what Oprah famously refers to as an aha! moment.

Once you have that moment of recognition, that aha! moment, act immediately. It is important to learn to make quick decisions once you receive the guidance you seek. Do not let anything stand in your way, not even money.

Money is almost always a barrier, but it is never a valid objection. This is what one of my colleagues, Karen Brook, says all the time. And she is 100 percent correct. The money will always follow and support your decision. So, no need to object, just accept the call and watch it appear.

This has worked for me and countless others. With each life coach I have worked with, I set a clear intention for what I wanted, and the money always manifested. Every. Single. Time. There is actually a law around this that I will teach you, should you choose to work with me. Just be sure to make the decision to go for it and remain dogged in your pursuit of what you want.

### 4. A Life Coach Who Can Identify and Teach You to Recognize Your Unique Qualities

The bottom line is that the job of a life coach is to hold the mirror up to your unique abilities and talents. If you feel anything other than unique and bursting with potential when you interview with a potential life coach, keep looking.

Each of us is a miracle with endless potential bottled up inside, waiting to pop the cork and set it free. So, dismiss anything or anyone who tells you or makes you feel otherwise. (This doesn't just apply to life coaches!)

The coaches I worked with always made me feel like I was one of the most amazing human beings they had ever met! They said it with such sincerity that I was able to believe them, which was and will always be important. The best part is that, now, I hold the same belief about myself that they held of me. I *know* I am a powerful creator! As are you!

It is our job to align ourselves with the right mentor (i.e., life coach) and the right information that will set us free to live the life of our choosing.

Find the life coach who believes in you and your abilities wholeheartedly. Find the life coach that makes you feel like you are a unique miracle exploding with potential. Why? First of all, because it's true. And second of all, because you deserve the best—the best life coach and the best that life has to offer.

By assuring the life coach you choose has ass-kicking qualities, you are prepared to take charge of your life, your destiny.

## Chapter Seven

# WHY YOU THINK YOU MAY NOT NEED A LIFE COACH

I believe everyone needs a life coach; however, you may not be ready for one. Here are some clues that you are not ready to work with a life coach.

*Warning: content below contains some hard truths that may sting when you read them!*

- **You still feel you can make it on your own.** You may be at a point in your life where you truly think you can make these changes on your own. You may agree that everyone needs support, that we are social beings by nature, and as such, require the help of others in order to rise. You may even know how much you need fresh ideas and energy to fuel your transformation. But you may not be convinced that you need that help just yet.

- **You still don't know where your life is heading.** This is perfectly normal. You may be unclear about what direction you want your life to take, so taking direction from someone may feel awkward and invasive. You might be asking, how can someone else help me with the direction in my life when I am not clear on what I want for my future? This is completely understandable. However, a life coach actually possesses the skills to help you connect with what you want to create in your future. When you do commit to the journey of becoming who you are meant to be, it is important to know that you are in good hands with the life coach you choose. And when you feel that comfort, you will know you are ready. So, no worries! Don't blame yourself for not knowing where you want to go or not feeling quite ready. The right mentor or coach will show up in your life just at the right time. Remember, when the student is ready, the teacher appears.

- **You can't commit to a life coach right now.** As I have stated emphatically throughout this book, working with a life coach requires a commitment of both time and effort. Whether you are preoccupied with completing your degree, raising children, or working long hours at a current job, your lifestyle, at this stage, may simply not allow enough free time to commit to a life coaching program. If this is you, know that the time will be right soon. However, ask yourself if you are making excuses. Truly, it only takes an hour a day of consistent effort to propel your life in a whole new direction. It is worth the sacrifice in the long run. We will always have time for the things that are important to us. Decide what is important to you and allot time, accordingly. Just make sure you are your top priority. If you legitimately do not have the time, make a promise to take the opportunity to work with a life coach as soon as your situation changes.

- **You are still not convinced that you can have and are worthy of having anything you want.** Low self-esteem and doubt are crippling for all of us. There may be nothing anyone can say or do that will allow you to see your worth. But do it anyway. You could try working with a life coach for a short period of time and see if they spark something inside you. My guess is once you get a taste of what your life can be like and who you can become with dedicated support by your side, you will want more.

- **You are not ready to give up who you are now.** Maybe you can't stop wanting to please others;

maybe you want to keep partying, or hooking up with guys, or just "having fun." Fair enough. When you work with a life coach, you will become a different person, and all of those old drives will likely fall away. Some people, quite frankly, are not ready to let go of who they are presently in order to embrace the person they can become. After all, being you as you are now is familiar and comfortable. You will only know you are ready to embrace the potential of the new you when the pain of the current you becomes unbearable. When you hit the unbearable bottom, don't delay. Get yourself a life coach and take one step at a time to build a new you and a new future.

- **You are happy enough just the way you are and with your life as it is.** Ain't nothin' wrong with that if you are able to acknowledge that every external condition in your life has an inward cause. The cause for unhappiness, discontent, or struggle—as well as their opposites—lies within you and not outside of you. Again, there is absolutely nothing wrong with not being ready to work with a life coach, but if you have read this far into the book, you might as well jump in and try it out. I can't speak for all coaching programs, but I can speak for mine. You will never look back. By committing just one hour a day to your growth and development, you will need a telescope to look back at your life by the end of the coaching term.

## The Challenge: It's Time to Get Real!

One of my favorite stories is *The Velveteen Rabbit* by Margery Williams. The stuffed rabbit wants to become real. He's observed that older toys, like the Skin Horse, have become real, so he asks, "What is real?" The Skin Horse's reply is that "It's a thing that happens to you [and that] it doesn't happen all at once." It's about being loved for a long time, really loved for what you are, even if "your eyes drop out and you get loose in the joints and very shabby. But these things don't matter at all, because once you are Real you can't be ugly, except to people who don't understand."

Your dream life awaits you. Would you like to know how to become real? It starts with knowing what you want and finding people who understand.

## Chapter Eight

# WHAT DO YOU WANT?

As stated earlier, one of the most important attributes a life coach offers is a program, and if they don't have one, my advice is to look for a different life coach.

The life coach program I've developed has a strong research foundation and offers unique perspectives and solutions, including a five-part visioning process that takes clients into themselves to define and refine exactly what they want:

- Connection
- It's Already Inside You
- Cleansing
- Making the Way
- The Decision

Take each section a day at a time. Read through the section, connect to yourself, and complete the exercises in the section titled "For Today's Journey."

## Day One: Connection

Here it is. The beginning of a new week, a new day—and if you choose—a whole new life, a whole new you. Yes, you, the one reading this—this is the birth of a *new you*!

Before you dismiss the idea, know that there is a reason you are reading this right now. There are no coincidences.

I am inviting you to explore the possibility that there is a *new you* trying to emerge, that you've caught glimpses of your inner struggle from time to time, but you are not sure what the struggle is about really or how to emerge on the other side.

Let me explain. That struggle will continue until you commit to discovering who you are as a passenger on an inner journey. That passenger is seeking awareness.

Your struggle results from your lack of awareness.

So, I'm asking: are you ready to journey to a place you've never gone before? A place that exists in all of us, no matter where we live, our religion, our sexual orientation or gender, or our financial resources. This place exists! Many go to their grave having never found this part of themselves. That is why I've written this book, hopefully in a way that will connect with the authentic part of you that keeps searching.

Here's the truth: That place inside of you is yours alone. It is not someone else's. Someone else cannot find it for you. You must find it for yourself.

You have things you want to accomplish, things you want to do, yet you question your ability to accomplish them. You dismiss your new ideas so quickly you didn't even realize they were there. You felt them, thought them, and dismissed them. Why?

What are you afraid of?

It is time to let yourself see things from a different perspective. I want you to open a door, even if it is a tiny crack, to your heart. That's right, just a smidgen. Close your eyes, peek inside. See inside your heart at what has been patiently waiting to be discovered, the part of yourself that has everything you will ever need.

Inside this place, in your heart of hearts, lies the power to transform your life so radically that others may not recognize you. All you have to do is dare to enter.

Leave behind your worries and doubts that are there due to your past experiences. Let go of all the shame and guilt. Let go of everything and anything that has happened.

You can open this door. Begin a new way of living. Begin living without limitations. No matter what has happened in the past, you can put it behind you, if you connect with what *you really, truly want.*

You can have the life you truly want if you can begin seeing things as they really are and not how you have been conditioned to see them. Stop fighting with the outer world, stop resisting your inner world. Go inward. Go inward to find the peace, inspiration, rejuvenation, nurturing, enlightenment, and strength needed to connect yourself with what you *really, truly want*. That is the first step.

### For Today's Journey

For today's journey, listen to music while you settle into yourself. [3] Spend a few minutes visualizing your heart, then visualize the heart inside your heart. Connect with what you really want in your heart of hearts. Find the way to make those desires a reality. Trust the process. Envision a door. Envision cracking it open and a bright beam of light shining through. Listen to the music while you visualize. Connect yourself to yourself. Relax. Enjoy.

## Day Two: It's Already Inside You

The next essential thing is to be truly honest with yourself. This isn't easy. Being honest about where you have been, where you are today, and what habits and addictions got you here is important. Being honest about where you want to go is *paramount*.

Inside yourself is another you that wants to come out and play. How often have you denied yourself that opportunity? Or translated it into behaviors that numbed you, dumbed you, made you succumb to others' needs and wants?

---

3 I suggest listening to "Primavera" by Ludovico Einaudi, which you can find on YouTube here: https://youtu.be/lTq2Iuyk1s8.

*For Today's Journey*

I have a simple yet powerful exercise for you that picks up where you were in the last exercise. I'm inviting you to do three things.

Be still.

Be quiet.

Go within.

Go to your heart of hearts. Look inside the door you've barely opened. See the light you've let shine through. This is where your deepest desires lie, those that you have been hiding from others, hiding from yourself, and hiding from the world. Let those desires come out and play.

Don't think. Feel. Let yourself dwell in what you *want*. No expectations or judgment. Feel what you want.

Now, write down at least three things that come to mind. Whatever pops into your mind, write it down. Write down things you have never told anyone. Write down things you may never tell anyone. Write from your heart of hearts what you want.

Don't judge these desires. Don't turn away from these parts of yourself. Do not deny or label these desires. What is within you is there for your good.

Let them flow into you naturally and easily; let them float through your mind and infuse your body with joy, gratitude, and peace.

Write them down.

## Day Three: Cleansing

Now that you have journeyed into your heart of hearts, given names to your desires, allowed your wants to flow through you, and written them down, what is next?

It's time to address all those feelings, wants, and desires in a safe and loving way. Not addressing your feelings is the greatest obstacle in life. You've kept this part of yourself closed off, in the dark. Now I'm telling you to keep this part of yourself open, yet safe.

The only way to do this is to open up both that which you feel hinders or hurts you, and also that which heals and blesses you. Acknowledging all of it is vitally important.

It's difficult addressing feelings, needs, and wants that hinder and hurt us. We don't want to. It's human nature to keep them buried, to deny them and not let them out.

Keeping them in the dark has not helped, though, has it? That's because living fully and opening to ourselves requires free-flowing energy. So, it is important for you to address these feelings safely, honestly.

What does this mean?

It requires you to accept your fear, sorrow, grief, anger, and trauma and then release them. You can't let these feelings out if you deny their presence. They must be released if you are to transform, to achieve your higher good.

If held inside or explicitly denied (as most of us have done for most our lives), these feelings will fester and boil and spill over into all parts of your life. You will hold them in your body where they present as illness, discomfort, and disease. They are toxic. They will pulse all over your body without you knowing, but you still feel them. When you hold them captive or deny their existence, they feed on you—your confidence, your health, your hopes. They will close the door you just opened that holds the healing power of transformation, keeping your flow of life choked off, resulting in illness, discomfort, and disease.

Your heart of hearts will close tightly if you do not address these toxic wants and needs in the right manner. If addressed correctly, these feelings will deepen your relationship with your heart of hearts and reveal a truth that only they can tell you.

## For Today's Journey

Flow into your heart of hearts. Be aware of both the dark and the light. Rejoice in what you have both within and without. Be grateful and pleased with all the undeniable joy you have in you and around you.

Now, pay special attention to the murky feelings, the feelings you've hidden. Look at those feelings that are not ideal, that are unwanted. They want to be seen. See them with compassion and understanding. See them. Gently notice them. Observe them and calmly acknowledge them.

Name them. Write them down, each and every one.

Once you've written them down, sit in a calm, quiet location and visualize your heart of hearts just as you did that first day. Open the door again and peer in at this beautiful heart. Notice its rhythmic beating, its perfect shape. And ask aloud, "How do I heal this? What are these feelings trying to show me that I don't want to see?"

Write down the first thought that comes to mind. That first voice is the voice of your true self contained within your heart of hearts. That is the part of you that holds the answers. It is this first voice that wants and needs to be heard by you, the voice that comes without conscious thought, before you begin to analyze the situation. That first voice has the answer. Listen.

Do not let analysis paralysis enter.

Just write out the first thing that comes to your mind. Stay present in this place with your heart of hearts open and relaxed, knowing it will tell you what you need to hear. Write what comes to mind. Let it pour out on to your paper.

Now, sit at peace with what you have learned. Breathe deeply, in and out, for a few minutes. Feel what you are feeling. Acknowledge the truths you have discovered. Mentally hug your heart of hearts and thank it for being open and honest with you.

You have now taken the time to connect and cleanse. You feel a new strength and understand that inside of you is the power to transform any situation for good. You are now ready to move forward to the life you have always wanted, with the faith that you have what it takes. If further work is needed, you will know what to do. You will know the next right step. The new you is ready to emerge.

# Day Four: Making the Way

When we are getting into our heart of hearts, we are making a connection to the higher version of ourself. It can be helpful to view this relationship as you would a parent to a child, yet inversely so. In our physical world, the parent is the person of authority who guides the child. Learning to inverse this relationship within ourselves is to truly free ourselves. In this inverse relation, the heart of hearts is the child. And remember, the heart of hearts has the power to transform your life.

As we mature, we forget our childlike wonder, dreams, and desires. We have lost or given away the freedom to see from within.

By flipping the relationship, our child self has the power to transform and lead us. The parent's job is to listen, nurture, appreciate, and love the child.

## For Today's Journey

Focus on an image that allows you to connect with the innermost part of yourself—the child within. Picture yourself as a child, pure and carefree, holding all the possibilities of the world. Your current age or life experiences don't matter. This child is still within you wanting to come out, light the way, and transform your life.

Go within to your heart of hearts with the vision of yourself as a child. The door is opening. See that part of yourself that has remained untouched by everything you have experienced. See your purity. You may have kept it hidden so it would stay safe, and today, it is safe. Today it knows you will listen, nurture, and appreciate all it has to say. Today it is the deepest part of yourself that you discover and adore.

## Day Five: The Decision

Wow! You did it. You took time to connect to your heart of hearts. You learned how to be still, go inward, and listen to what your first voice has to say. You accepted you have the power to transform unwanted situations into lessons. You rediscovered your pure, childlike wonder. You learned it will show you the way if you listen. Congratulations! Just one more step.

Getting quiet and connecting is essential in strengthening this bond and building a relationship and dialogue with your heart of hearts. It always speaks with emotions.

The things you desire are the things you will use to move toward. The things that cause you to close off are the things you want to move away from.

The first day you wrote down your desires. This last day, now that you have cleared the way and connected to your heart of hearts, it is time to let it all pour out.

*For Today's Journey*

Be still. Listen to your voice telling you what you want. Write down every single desire you have within.

Once you have written it all down, decide on one that you want more than any other. Go deep within. Go for it!

Once you've made the decision, write down how you envision this playing out. It can be your perfect day, as if the desire has already materialized. Or it can be a moment in time in which you are being recognized and rewarded. The important thing is that once you have decided, you must make a commitment to yourself to do one thing that will make your desire a reality. Right now.

- Write down another thing you can do in 24 hours
- Commit and repeat the next 24 hours
- See how long it takes for your desire to materialize once you start focusing
- Do one thing once a day toward realizing your deepest desire

That is not too much to ask. It is not too much to do in order to move into a new future. The new you.

It is simple, easy, and fun. You see, life is a game. You just have to learn how to play, how to find your joy by reaching for the thing you most desire and making it happen. You are the creator of your own instruction manual. For free downloadable PDF of this five part visioning process, please visit www.barbarajoyce.com.

Chapter Nine

# The End...
# and the Beginning

Dear Reader,

This book contains simple advice and solid reasons for seeking a life coach, all so you can become the best possible *you*. Just in case you need to be reminded, here are the reasons.

- You are worth it
- You deserve the best
- Healing and success are your birthright
- The world needs the real you

The world doesn't need any more imposters. The world needs more authentic people living lives full of passion, purpose, and playfulness. We need people who are deeply happy and fulfilled. We need teams and tribes and counsels of these people working together for the greater good. We need the real you!

The real you is here for a reason at this specific point in time.

Becoming real is the journey we engage in with a life coach. It is what has happened for me and countless others. I, too, have become real. A real human being, a real woman, a real friend. A real life coach, passionate about helping you. I have shed the masks, and I see who I really am. I am a real human endowed with a creative essence that is bursting at the seams to show others the way to this truth.

While this concludes my book, I hope it marks the beginning of a very special journey for you. I am not an expert at everything, but I certainly know what worked for me. I know what works for countless others, too. It would be an honor to accompany you on your journey to find what works for you.

Blessings,

Barbara

www.barbarajoyce.com

www.instagram.com/barbarajoycelive

www.facebook.com/iambarbarajoyce

# EPILOGUE

Barbara Joyce's *Ditch the Boyfriend and Get a Life Coach* is the book for you, IF you want to grow and succeed beyond your wildest dreams. I have had many life coaches over the years, and I have achieved tremendous success. Having a life coach is the best gift you can give yourself, especially if you are stuck.

Barbara's suggestions on making sure you get the right life coach will help you get unstuck, discover your real self, and recognize your worth. An authentic person living a life full of passion, purpose, playfulness and success, Barbara is the best! Her proven methods and resources are for anyone wanting to live life full out, reach their full potential and realize their personal worth.

This book and her coaching process will help you be the real you, because you deserve the best. And the world needs the best you possible.

– Tessa Greenspan, Entrepreneur and
Best-Selling Author of *From Outhouse to Penthouse*

# Appendix A

# Barbara's Favorite Resources

The following resources will get you started on your journey. Some are articles or books that I read while writing this book. Others are meditations or more recent publications and will help you along your way. I highly recommend digging into them and enjoying the process of opening your mind.

## Books:

1. *You Were Born Rich* by Bob Proctor
2. *As a Man Thinketh* by James Allen
3. *Think and Grow Rich* by Napoleon Hill
4. *Your Invisible Power* by Geneviève Behrend
5. *Everything Is Figureoutable* by Marie Forleo
6. *Ask and It Is Given* by Esther and Jerry Hicks

## Articles:

1. "How Life Coaching Works and How It Can Benefit You Today" https://www.tonyrobbins.com/coaching/results-life-coach/
2. "20 Born to Coach Personality Traits All Great Coaches Share" https://www.evercoach.com/blog/20-born-to-coach-personality-traits-all-great-coaches-share
3. "Why Everyone Needs a Life Coach" https://greatist.com/happiness/why-everyone-needs-a-life-coach#1

## YouTube Favorites:

1. *SuperSoul Conversations* with Jack Canfield: https://youtu.be/-AFJMgcuJBw
2. "How to Achieve Your 'Impossible' Dreams" with Marie Forleo and Dr. Tererai Trent: https://youtu.be/Ewh1zT8VpQo
3. "Calm Guided Meditation to Gain Abundance, Love & Happiness" by Bob Proctor: https://www.youtube.com/watch?v=lssNBHXz4Vw
4. "Serenity," an excerpt from the book *As a Man Thinketh* by James Allen, read by Rodney Ronquillo: https://youtu.be/r6RBE_OPDlw
5. Abraham Hicks on law of attraction: https://www.youtube.com/watch?v=V0MtWvPT1Ys&t=514s

## Appendix B

# LIFE COACH INTERVIEW CHECKLIST

| Qualities | Coach 1 | Coach 2 | Coach 3 | Notes |
|---|---|---|---|---|
| Compassionate | | | | |
| Supportive | | | | |
| Grateful | | | | |
| Positive | | | | |
| Curious | | | | |
| Observant | | | | |
| Great Listener | | | | |
| Excellent communicator | | | | |
| Courageous | | | | |
| Humble | | | | |
| Focused | | | | |
| Dedicated | | | | |
| Professional | | | | |
| Honest | | | | |
| Trustworthy | | | | |
| Sincere | | | | |

| Qualities | Coach 1 | Coach 2 | Coach 3 | Notes |
|---|---|---|---|---|
| Learning Machine | | | | |
| Innovative | | | | |
| Worthy of modeling | | | | |
| Uses a program with proven outcomes | | | | |
| Has keen Intuition | | | | |
| Can connect with you | | | | |
| Can identify and help you grow your unique qualities | | | | |

# Acknowledgments

It took three years and a village to convince me to publish this book. Thank you to my Mom for being there for me through it all, my sister Sandra who understands me and still loves me, and my sister Sue for seeing me for who I truly am. Thank you especially to my children Alexa, Ellie, and Mikey for your strength and resilience as I struggled through some very tough years and very tough topics. You are infinitely resilient, and every day, I admire your tenacity and courage.

To all my sisters in 12-step meetings, thank you for your love and support. I would never have known what true friendship was without you.

Thank you also for the women mentioned in this book who hold a special place in my life: my childhood friend Kristin Boyer Snodgrass and Stacy Oliver, my friend who saved me from the depths of myself.

Thank you specifically to Tina Permann for being my pure inspiration to coach others. A special thank you to Bob Proctor for your infinite wisdom and your passion to share this information that changes lives forever. Tessa Greenspan, thank you for encouraging me to follow my passion and for our unbelievable talks. To my team of inspiration who are helping me see more of me: Barbara Condron and Paul Pilva. I become more of myself every day with your guidance and support. To all the PGI consultants and my coaching friends, let's keep changing the world one person at a time!

To my current team encouraging me with your gentle (and sometimes firm) nudges to create my own program, thank you for seeing and loving all of me. To my first editor, Vesna Zuban, thank you for believing in me and this message. To my current editor, Cheryl Roberts Oliver, thank you for truly seeing this message for what it is and for honoring its importance. You have an absolute gift for being in the energy of the book and bringing it to life. To Adela Martinez Camacho and Barb Wagner for bringing my book cover design to life. And to Cathy Davis, you are a magician when it comes to books. I am so grateful for your patience and your wisdom and your phenomenal team! This book is published because of you.

# About the Author

Barbara Joyce is a Women's Empowerment Coach. Following her passion in personal development, she empowers women to find their voices and take steps in creating the life they desire. No stranger to failure and disappointment, Barbara realizes much of being a coach is about lifting the client up and creating an atmosphere of trust and understanding. It is about expanding who they are as individuals to create a stronger bond with what they already know to be true inside. She knows from personal experience, that having that one person in life who we trust makes all the difference in the world. Barbara wants to be that person who guides her clients to freedom.

By creating an atmosphere of trust, Barbara helps women identify what pain points and obstacles inhibit them from achieving true freedom. By addressing these subconscious beliefs and habits, she helps clients create a stronger bond with their true selves and share their unique talents with the world. This results in ultimately freeing them to be not only who they want to be, but also who they are designed to be. Barbara believes that we all have a purpose and she is committed to helping each client find theirs.

iambarbarajoyce@gmail.com
www.barbarajoyce.com/coaching/
www.facebook.com/iambarbarajoyce
www.instagram.com/barbarajoycelive/
www.twitter.com/babsjoyce
www.linkedin.com/in/barbara-joyce-23601712/

www.ingramcontent.com/pod-product-compliance
Lightning Source LLC
Chambersburg PA
CBHW060327130626
46553CB00003B/940